The Name of This
Intersection Is Frost

The Name of This Intersection Is Frost

Maryrose Larkin

Shearsman Books
Exeter

First published in the United Kingdom in 2010 by
Shearsman Books Ltd
58 Velwell Road
Exeter EX4 4LD

www.shearsman.com

ISBN 978-1-84861-117-7
First Edition

Acknowledgements
Pieces of the following have appeared, in differing forms, in
*Fascicle, Gutcult, Hubbub, No Tell Motel, Shearsman,
St. Elizabeth Street,* and *Take Out.*

Inverse was published as a chapbook
by nine muses books in 2006.

Contents

For Eric

Inverse

Roots open   rise and run
         his face *compare to*   string notation

                    logic
             required and where

but this cannot   and without it
box step   the sun and   box step   the moon

Elements consecrate the charting

      the state of
      the imperfect forgotten
      wanting afterward
      and

           see also elsewhere

A vital mark   a result

    archaic
    an
    abundance
    poured out

Abundance in form and iodine to
                    never half hollow muscular reflect

        surface clutched and stung

                        compare to
        factory as peony glimpsed

Usually with little or no connotation

or	the	calendar	inverse	
	a hinge	serving	as	subject

precise numbers
    a platen of beautiful peculiar

.

Come and absolve the resistance

                          come chance tides

come   expound   breath intelligible
come shine
come abound unfold in   and about go

The name of this intersection is frost broken up

heavy spar reign   heavy phrase ravishment
                       strands careening

let us unfurl instead: weather
                 see also river

   see also   self   and the less restricted sense

When she was younger
her limbs a passage *or*

           four to encircle not to ghost
           four to collate:
chaos moon   chaos fist   door   chaos fact

Grove hold

        suggests his branches were fashioned into legs

and she was said to be   alphabet ends fastened

no   she
       was misspelled   as noose

My missing princess pillow book
             posit not locate

azalea into queen's lace
center into hour

or

garden to Hudson
                    I wave

It depicts   grief or
       surrender emissions

      translates push
         divisions opposing

             akin to
             yield or
             become altered

destroy a gradual picture gradually

  (process of

paint circumstance charge

    the current process is to take or catch
the array's first element: castle take or castle catch

A verb
to disguise failure

        archaic   rampant
        flustered vital
        lavish disorder

suggests often exceeding jumbled *suggests* often-bountiful mistakes

Ache faced moon
doubled and
younger

      stammered up
      fist as fact

see also
and the moon in war and after

Payment of form to form the transfer   vary vessel

image composites   :   flowerhead
                         cut flat on the reflection

        compare to dismantle

Sing in and the computer responds rupture

    between characters
             and currents sing in

or

    between theories waking life
    ached direction holy and punctuate

sing in
over language sing   out

See send   *see* journey   *see*

         the opposite surface
double strands rooted : road map or

it may be described as outer one some closed inner
         as tactile point

compare to   internal ascents

Or out
    remembered into drop serene shaking
        shadow sung and shadow grey

pansy rime encased not knowing and then
damaged wanting   noise at the end of the mind

Telephone and type

        contentious

        the reader *as in* the danger
        last ladder plunge head first

    wrap around
    this recent life   and

It flickers and
        mistakes pour   forth

                       a riotous   primer
                  where a and b are constants

   synonyms: flicker   fusion frequency

Photocopy of the year's ghost curve :

paradise	interlace	velocity
addition	closed	patter

press alphabet

what it teaches it teaches at random

A   stanza   performed   by

      elaborate patterning *or* detrimental
         intensity *or* an unfavorable metric row

        an anthem
      extracted against stem   or   axis

Wilder to   half mirror
                pebbles   to   pivot heart

Possible   *compare to*
     sanctuary   coil

          severed

     compulsion   *compare to*
     frame by   frame

Before disorder
            confused tumble blooming or wanting

ornament rays loose and opposite
petals marked by sequence of belonging to
            this genus chance america of *of*

see also   anagram the human oxide
see also   nomenclature grey textbloom

compare to articulate silicate *compare to* countersign
                          to the tongue flowering

Late Winter 30

The pressure of facing the why section when I wanted horizon
pressure dropped winter angle face and spring 50%   pushed
through grey replacing from the top and patchy chaos

       no   winter or   late winter
                                   shiver cover *some can never*

late one in whirl no opposite morning cross struck pink
change insoluble atmosphere east facing mothering under
but not mother not cinders not mocking pushed into wings

suffer late other petal synoptic surface shadow and 50% *no* 30%
no 30 pansies silver light on the fenceline
                                      rain the written

Line slope watch gray lit sidelines   why

color awake 30 rouse throated blooms

in visible   scattered daffodils   rusted layers

sea and why   wing section   spring visible

face or mocking heart   the grasping

silver winter awake her hearts ease cinder

day eye ash cross scattered rouse white

elegy burned blue morning not heaven pushed

still not blooming petals violet   late 30

Winter mocking
bird   curved cedar   opposite

        and early ash
        white shadow impossible shivering frond gray

                my   mocking
document : a garden
        late facing each when facing late face
        stratus violet north or

an expecting change crossed and the   other changes
                        rusted and mapeye

Viol throated the   opposite suffer

cross sun stations no inner   jonquil limbed

still   petals   under layers

violet   a late 30 change tide   *no*
why   her visible section scattered   bare

cirrostratus temperature   fenced sky system awake

Ruin from one mother too late or silver early crows south on the chain link others bloomed when and from winter this chance

section replacing late whirl change not petal not written not stratus   I have no other missions clearly inserted 50% scrim crossed classified layers frond drift

winter is the 50% change cinders 50% starling face and rage eye bare chance mapped as change why frond cinders ease and silver fence

Grey ruination other and sun chance of dropped wings chaos scatter winter is ragged 30 documents and an invulnerable heart

Vast shadow   and still   limb
crossed   sections

           crocus inside

horizon   startle
                              late
                              cedar

           mapped a
           river singing 30

Chance weatherings   winter 30 missions   and horizon under
the crocus   here rage is inserted   clearly changes or angel
petal mother angle moth spring

and 50%   invisible   never here   where side drift south
anesthetic pink no river inner scrim to blue bare   haze
and grey blooming

        2 crossed the garden

either ruination or ruination fence   late scatter classification
rage is interested   crows pushing across the   steps

late sun change   winter classified into *never*   and   *never*
blue scatter prime rose   crow   yolk   winter hearted 4
limbed other sorrow signed

50%   petal aside spring

the 50% tide east

the wedding frond
 struck and sectioned

and life line rusted
in and change

weathering 50%

Velum throat   or   river throat

and startle early   a change   stuttered   under   the horizon
rhododendron awake- layers clearly   why   cross   yolk
why   closed   pink   a 50%   garden or   fence
lines   the chance   my frond   eyed curve expecting weather

or remain or rain or

cedar   vs winter I'll never   ruin a a late sun crocus   pushing
as a mission expecting cinder petals tide block dark limbs adrift
south south   perspective still documented still scrim winter
ruination

 wings or cirrostratus   or

shiver   suffer   no   blue sky tide   no stepping over the other
sunset fence all surface silver   spring is covering the visible not
to other inserted   struck   winter   thirty throated whip
to ash   and hazy late blooming   or limbed   or violet white

49

Look again: shadow chaos   train chaos   expecting   *never*

I'm partly a mouthpiece partially an other partly indifferent
          winter winter

dodger   cirrocumulus or every or suffer or mouth or late
thirty passed over doppler impossible she pushed into a
shadow and it pushed back

                don't look

partly partially   partly window   partly fractured inland
and in body and   system   partly mixing up and
pinked out

side sun   snow
cinder and sail   visible startle   pansy morning
sectioned   shadow   and dodge

why rage again   side silver   awake
light   upwards the

always visible   four
                  winter hearted ruinations
                  closed document   remains and

and impossible   thirty

passed over
backyard late   jay curved

horizon clearly   shiver layered and spring

Vast snow struck section pink mixed with light and drift

cinder and sail section pansy   pink persecution fence complex
hazy identity seized and grasping out   side layer late silver jay

I am unsettled under the action or under the influence of the
action or under the influence of pushing through yolk unhealed
and unlimbed hand mouth wing lung small and lung large

strange ascending   division starlings

whipping chance limbed to drift   fence seize and   heavy mixed
grasped with light and starlings in contact with ground rain   and
bitter change the west surface

relentless   delusions of the distant cedar   there's a 50% corolla
drift   divisible by the visible hand sky   strange struck mouth

sky lung sky scalloped awake hazy beforehand spring and
          written in and document out

Cerulean suffer   no visible morning   no sky and cross sun
pink petals on the   why section

50% or tide   layers rusted and snow limbed   under   she
         cirrostratus late temperature   chance

         when we awake hovere opposite   horizon
                  denominator fence or   document   why

and out again
and horizon
and violet violet unsettling
and rusted more
and in again
and change clearly
and no east winter
and no east river
and no cerulean thirty
and gone again

and petal that
and out again
and petal this
and atmosphere awake
and surface startle
and in again
and gone again
and yellow gray
and moving white

and denominator
and ruination
and out again
and
and in again
and shadow throat
and line life
and mission to
and chain link fence
and cinder faced
and gone again

I'll be the 50% chance

A visible morning sectioned into pink and temperature and
velum describing the green whip section scrim and system
bluish pressure wings dodger petals or rage

side silver moving suffer and   she dropped the impossible
never blooming no lines curved up pink 30 don't look or

spring faced or shiver why wing why it pushed back every
or suffer clearly why angel winter or sun chance yolk jay layer
side

  her mockingbird mouth out grasping and identity inserted

late silver train moving and up 4 winter awake- cirrocumulus
pushed side sun shiver cerulean suffer crocus cinder and sail
rhododendron chambers and startle camellia

Petal   aside
where late suffers   other petal
                violets   describing

no yearly mission

            winter crocus
spring is 50%   tide   pushing into
                east facing   under mothering

These impossible changes and the rose section through some atmosphere mocking inserted where and rage 4 petal singing under pink expecting the horizon 50% and some facing pushed and light petal south haze garden classification 4 vast crocus 30 the cross 50% garden lines eyed or cedar ruin to blooming sectioned scatter bird out

facing spring winter no and mocking frond and here invisible late sun yolk and cedar yolk my petals still no surface thirty or vulnerable I wanted spring to cover morning east mocking impossible late or and under angel invisible drift bare scatter singing under why never other visible throat 30 drift

Atmosphere north yolk

              and

the chance of drawing the 2 of a chance of facing
                   the 30   of why sections

and again and   and   chance of and   relentless

Wedding frond   haze and velum 2 were there but then a
cinderblock struck the primrose   other   *no never* never
another chance to and the late winter bloomed inside

closed up   and suffering invisible why a sidereal
morning   curved   internal cross no chance of sun   or
pansies why wing section   why suffer suffer or shiver
rhododendron

stratus and scrim documents: daffodil classified into early
push   late dark scatter hearted and broken yolk
cirrostratus late late   and   the scrim document says
that spring is covering up   the steps over the   ruination
fence

Rusted out and bluish and closed
shadow fronds and fence posts

station and cross scattered
rhododendron cinder   in the visible

east a crocus blooming
insides missing violets I miss

spring yolk fifty percent ruination
jonquil day an eye mapped limbs and ashes

impossible north except when impossible
here are 30 pictures of the sky

Of and late struck mother shadow written shivering facing
rusted crocus 50% to fence late crow shadow late early winter
cinder documented shiver all winder limbed scatter

crocus when grey can east into pansies cedar document or
winter changes drift blooming into limbed cross 30 horizon a
expecting late limbs wings no covering to sectioned

describing pressure pressure patchy *can* cross mothering into
50% on bird frond each expecting crocus mother anesthetic
and either and crow limbed shadow scatter inside

velum vs horizon   remain vs ruination

I replace east with documents or missions or drifts 2 inserted
never sorrow section velum garden remain sun adrift or the
hazy error

            Throated ruination
winter section river   weaker mother winter   winter mocking

layers moving north   curved sun   opposite   whirl
no in   temperature my   inner mocking document

chance of blooming lines weathering awake grey light on the

why angle   shadow   sidelines   why south   white impossible

        grayish crocus shiver frond grey   stretching
atmosphere north except when east   facing east or facing
stratus north   or petal late

yolk   more and   4   pansy late horizon   haze   and
        2 of fences and why and of other crosses and cinder
mapped   not expecting   I'm invisible

Curvature   my mocking lateral drift south anesthetic pink
the measures pressure face whirl morning crossed the
late suffer other document: enormous shadow   this

never and will never be that
petal and that and this petal and this surface rogue and they

insisted early stuttered or to stay or rain or these
missions are in cinders   thirty-sectioned winter across the
scatter unsettled side of the fence haze   hidden chaos or she

These 30 errors on the horizon

snow drift
scatter unsettle

no fence side haze
describing her heart as a mockingbird

partly ash partially crocus
partly vulnerable and sectioned out

Morning still   no internal sky and no cross   document
no inner   scatter bare blooming vulnerable and cumulus
constant beyond the fence

visible   cross   unsettle and describing   no   inner
thirty   missions

strata   rusted and   awake   and grey   and push limbed
system cinders and   sectioned

camellia describing 50% petals and   snowy morning
wild aside why

Winter morning and rain shadow   each under spring and
prime signed

pressure replacing some and patchy mothering chance never
this rain covers the impossible scalloped winter bitter heart

ruin tide   spring eye wedding side

I'm partly mocking and later partially mocking and then
mocking

dropped and no west document scatter river or as other no
bird inter patchy opposite on and moth either or no other
crocus lines cedar pressure not haze sorrow inside and tide *no*
no mother north startled snow facing not or grey this late drift

Scatter surface tides' 4 cinders today
cirrocumulus vs   describing

winter mocking the other partly partly cloudy flared

some blue sorrow some petal never some
          horizon 50%

 crocus 4 chambers and system shadow

Face grey my winter chance was this map and change folded
it up

winter crocus in ashes and no limbs documented

crossed   here moth late sorrow still bye bye facing winter
pushed late pink opposite   my face bloomed rage

blue   inserted on the error side
stepping   surface cross describes crocus

an angle through winter one not rain and mocking late and
spring is 2 rivers and 2 ruinations *never* yolk to petal cedar
river early awake-why the or no all spring haze partially

surface pansies   winter shadow and her garden rusted and
north prime hearted river is clearly weather I'll as tide snow
south as

North except when east

bird moving   curved cedar   opposite temperature
mocking   document   chance of bloom

lines weathering awake grey light   on the sidelines why

yolk   more and   late   ash   shadow

I'm impossible today shivering frond   stretching
          atmosphere   garden late   facing east

winter   section   river weaker mocking

late   facing   stratus   north violet   or   petal and
expecting change

eye cinder   and   cross   the other   changes   rusted and
          mapped eyed

Still morning pansy face   cinder stratus scrim   closed curved
bloom pink document bare suffer no power lines suffer   no
blue mission   suffer my   internal unsettled atmosphere no
sky eyed   facing east   to the visible and why haze late
winter thirty   why cross section rhododendron   why whirl
why not other/not mother   sorrowside sun wings velum or
river violet   lifting wild anesthetic shiver   inner life

2 daffodil   4 crocus she is not a garden   heart   and
cirrostratus covering expecting late winter   expecting
late winter dark yolk   blooming cinderblock a   scatter system
changing under :   ember crow   horizon   weds
time   struck early   frond   yearly crocus   late
primrose push scales moving   whip limbed   violet white
spring and temperature   inserted

the   winter's south tide   rusted shut   perspective   adrift
petal colored-awake and sunset sided   late and people remain
or rain or   weathering   cedar and horizon   I'll never
spring stretching in one step over   the other/mother fence
all surface and   silver ruination   a snow startle   a rage
petal   an ash throated denominator   or   opposite   fence
line a 50% chance of chance   or bluish or grayish   or
clearly struck

Maryrose Larkin lives in Portland, Oregon, where she works as a freelance researcher. She is the author of *Inverse* (nine muses books, 2006), *Whimsy Daybook 2007* (FLASH+CARD, 2006), *The Book of Ocean* (i.e. press, 2007) and *DARC* (FLASH+CARD, 2009). Maryrose is one of the organizers of Spare Room, a Portland-based writing collective, and is co-editor, with Sarah Mangold, of FLASH+CARD, a chapbook and ephemera poetry press.

www.ingramcontent.com/pod-product-compliance
Lightning Source LLC
Chambersburg PA
CBHW031932080426

42734CB00007B/650